Abundant Life Skills

Battle for the Mind

By
Stephen Matthew

D1143551

Abundant Life Publishing

(c) Stephen Matthew 2004

Abundant Life Publishing
Wapping Road, Bradford
West Yorkshire BD3 0EQ

First Published In 2004

Printed by:
Interprint Creative Solutions
Market Flat Lane, Knaresborough
North Yorkshire HG5 9JA

www.interprint-ltd.co.uk

British Library Cataloguing in Publication Data
A catalogue record for this book is available from the British library

ISBN: 0-9538516-3-X

Series Introduction

ABUNDANT LIFE SKILLS

Equipping you to live an abundant life

Jesus said: *'I came that they may have life, and have it abundantly' (John 10:10).* God's will is for every Christian to enjoy an abundant life on earth followed by an eternal life in heaven. It should just get better and better! But living it to the full takes skill and application.

In this series of Bible Studies we explore some of the Christian life skills that will equip you to live the abundant life Jesus gave you to the full. The truths examined and principles discussed are simply tools and must therefore be put to use. The more you use them, the more skilled you will become at living the abundant Christian life you know God has for you.

These studies are deliberately packed with God's Word. Most scriptures are written out in full as part of the text, so reading each lesson takes you on a Bible study through the subject. We have presented the material in this way because above all else, you need to know what God says about these subjects. It is then your responsibility to apply his Word and ways into your personal situation.

Abundant Life Skills can be used individually or for group study. At the close of each lesson you will find a few questions for discussion as well as some ideas about how to personally apply the truths to your life. There's also plenty of space at the end of each lesson for you to make your own notes as you read and think things through.

These studies will equip you with skills for abundant living and we are confident that as you apply them they will make a lasting impact on you, your friends, family, church and the wider community.

Stephen Matthew
Series Editor

Contents

LESSON 1 - You Are What You Think

LESSON 2 - Understanding the Battle

LESSON 3 - Taking Your Thoughts Captive

LESSON 4 - Developing a Faith Image

LESSON 5 - Maintaining Your faith image

LESSON 6 - Thinking As God Thinks

Lesson 1
YOU ARE WHAT YOU THINK

Have you ever seriously considered just what effect the way you think has on the way you live your life? It is a well-established fact that what goes on in the unseen reaches of your thought life has a direct impact on every area of your life. Your attitudes, hopes and fears, the way you speak, your personal philosophy of life, how you react to others, how you do your job and relate to your family, are all shaped by the way you think.

Out of his God-given wisdom Solomon encapsulated this principle in a single phrase:

'As a man thinks within himself, so he is.'
(Proverbs 23:7 NASB)

Every act, however good or bad, begins with a single thought.

1. It All Started with an Idea

A single thought can change your life dramatically if it is dwelt upon, developed and translated into action. Indeed, every modern convenience we have now began with an idea in the mind of the inventor! Equally, every facet of your character and action of your life started as a single thought. For example:

- The first sight of a man's future wife triggered a thought pattern which resulted in him asking for a date and their ultimate marriage.

- The first time a convict considered how easy it would be to shoplift, he triggered a thought pattern that resulted in him stealing and his eventual imprisonment.

- The idea of people being able to fly like a bird triggered a sequence of events that resulted in the development of the aeroplane.

- The child's first encounter with a barking dog set off a thought pattern which resulted in a deep-seated fear of being attacked by one even in adult life.

This principle can work either positively for our good or negatively for our harm.

a. Positive

'Just then a woman who had been subject to bleeding for twelve years came up behind him and touched the edge of his cloak. She said to herself, "If I only touch his cloak, I will be healed." Jesus turned and saw her. "Take heart, daughter," he said, "your faith has healed you."' (Matthew 9:20-22)

What motivated this sick woman to push through the crowd to reach Jesus? A single thought: 'If only I touch his cloak, I will be healed.' She had no doubt heard about and perhaps even seen others healed by Jesus. This rekindled the dying hope that she would one day be well again. She *had* to touch him. If only she could, she just *knew* she would be healed. This thought, which had now become a confidence of faith, gripped and motivated her as she pushed through the crowd. Nothing would stop her - and she received according to her faith.

A single thought, based on the truth of God's desire to heal the sick, triggered the whole sequence of events leading to its realisation.

b. Negative

'One evening David got up from his bed and walked around on the roof of the palace. From the roof he saw a woman bathing. The woman was very beautiful and David sent someone to find out about her. The man said, "Isn't this Bathsheba, the daughter of Eliam and the wife of Uriah the Hittite?" Then David sent messengers to get her. She came to him, and he slept with her.'
(2 Samuel 11:2-4)

Note the sequence of events that took place here:

1. He saw

What he saw - probably quite innocently and by accident - entered his mind and started a chain reaction which he could have stopped at any time.

2. He considered

He considered what he saw, pondered the woman's beauty and allowed his mind to dwell on her until what had been an accidental glance became lustful thoughts.

3. He enquired

His thoughts resulted in an enquiry into who she was as his train of thought rolled on unchecked.

4. He entertained her

His request to meet her now had only one purpose behind it - to satisfy the lust triggered by that initial thought.

David's thought became an act. The way he had thought within himself was the way he had become. A lustful thought became an act of adultery.

2. You Are in Charge

The sad truth is that the sequence could have been stopped at any point if David had so desired. He was the master of his own thoughts - as are we of ours.

'We demolish arguments and every pretension that sets itself up against the knowledge of God, and we take captive every thought to make it obedient to Christ.'
(2 Corinthians 10:5)

Recognising this truth should cause us as responsible Christians to take control of our thought lives. A sinful thought that is not dealt with will result in a sinful action. On the other hand, a righteous thought that is entertained will produce righteous actions:

'Those who live according to the sinful nature have their minds set on what that nature desires; but those who live in accordance with the spirit have their minds set on what the Spirit desires.'
(Romans 8:5)

This scripture describes how the nature of your life - expressed in actions, speech and attitudes - is a consequence of where your mind is 'set'. The fixing of your mind on a matter is an issue of personal choice. You decide whether or not to entertain in your mind thoughts that you know are sinful. You have the final say as to what you fill your mind with. So:

'Set your mind on things above, not on earthly things.'
(Colossians 3:2)

3. Your Mind and Your Salvation

Does this then mean that by a thought process, I can bring myself into God's favour and so obtain salvation? No! The principle of fixing your mind on something works for everyone, whether they are inside or outside of Christ. It is a creation law, established by God for all humanity. Our challenge as Christians is to recognise this and make the principle work for us as we seek to develop into the people God is calling us to be.

a. A spiritual experience

Our new birth is primarily a spiritual issue. In order to be born again our natural mind must lay aside its logic and reason and submit to God's Word and the operation of simple faith. Nicodemus, in his encounter with Jesus, was confronted with this dilemma. Jesus said to him:

'"Unless a man is born again, he cannot see the kingdom of God." "How can a man be born when he is old?" Nicodemus asked. "Surely he cannot enter a second time into his mother's womb to be born!" Jesus answered, 'I tell you the truth, unless a man is born of water and the Spirit, he cannot enter the kingdom of God. Flesh gives birth to flesh, but the Spirit gives birth to spirit."'
(John 3:3-6)

Nicodemus had to come to a place of seeing that salvation was not a matter of simply doing right or thinking right. It was a matter of receiving by faith the gift of eternal life that God offers:

'It is by grace you have been saved, through faith - and this not from yourselves, it is the gift of God.'
(Ephesians 2:8)

b. A complete transformation

Our salvation, though a spiritual encounter initially, deals with the whole of our being - body, soul and spirit. The work of the Holy Spirit permeates every department of our lives:

'If anyone is in Christ, he is a new creation; the old has gone, the new has come!'
(2 Corinthians 5:17)

The process of change which takes place in our life after coming to Christ (known as sanctification) affects every part of us. It is a process of change towards a very specific goal:

'We... are being transformed into [Christ's] likeness with ever-increasing glory, which comes from the Lord, who is the Spirit.'
(2 Corinthians 3:18)

c. Co-operating with Christ

Our salvation was initiated by God in his grace and we received our new birth as a free gift by faith, knowing that there was nothing we could do to merit or earn it. Our ongoing Christian experience, however, is not passive or beyond our control. We have a responsible part to play.

We are by nature creatures of free will and choice. As a Christian I can choose to disobey God or to follow him wholeheartedly. While God works in me, my responsibility is to outwork in the practical areas of my life his purpose and will for me:

'Continue to work out your salvation with fear and trembling, for it is God who works in you to will and to act according to his good purpose.'
(Philippians 2:12-13)

A major part of 'working out' what God has done in us begins by thinking correctly. The way we think as Christians and what we let our minds dwell upon has a great bearing on our spiritual growth and stability.

4. Get Out of the Mould

Our responsibility to think right as we work out what God has put in us is seen in the following scripture:

'Do not conform any longer to the pattern of this world, but be transformed by the renewing of your mind.'
(Romans 12:2)

Because we live in the fundamentally godless society we were brought up in, our minds have become conditioned to its way of thinking. Humanism, rationalism and atheism permeate much of the educational and social fabric of the western world today. This inevitably works against God's purpose for us. If we continue to think according to the pattern of this world we become like all the other people in the world who are *'Without hope and without God in the world' (Ephesians 2:12)*.

We can change. We can break out of this world's mould. We can be transformed into people who know and do God's will and represent Christ perfectly. How? By the renewing of our minds.

5. Renewing Your Mind

God's ultimate purpose for us is to be like Christ; we must therefore think the way Christ thinks. This involves a deliberate act of our will on two counts. First, we need to decide not to *'conform any longer to the pattern of this world' (Romans 12:2).* This is the mental choice, the introduction of a new way of thinking. Then follows a decision to act in line with this new way of thinking. We deliberately decide not to do the things which characterised the life we once lived in the world before we came to Christ. We need to say: 'I won't conform to the pattern of this world - I'm going to think God's thoughts and consequently live God's way.'

'Set your minds on things above, not on earthly things. For you died and your life is now hidden with Christ in God... Put to death, therefore, whatever belongs to your earthly nature: sexual immorality, impurity, lust, evil desires and greed, which is idolatry. Because of these, the wrath of God is coming. You used to walk in these ways, in the life you once lived. But now you must rid yourself of all such things as these: anger, rage, malice, slander and filthy language from your lips. Do not lie to each other, since you have taken off your old self with its practices and have put on the new self, which is being renewed in knowledge in the image of its Creator.'
(Colossians 3:2-3, 5-10)

As we set our minds to think God's way we will also be able to put to death, or 'rid ourselves' of our old sinful life patterns:

'In the same way, count yourselves dead to sin but alive to God in Christ Jesus. Therefore do not let sin reign in your mortal body so that you obey its evil desires. Do not offer the parts of your body to sin, as instruments of wickedness.'
(Romans 6:11-13)

'Counting' or 'reckoning' ourselves dead to sin is an issue to do with the mind. Consider, think, ponder, meditate upon the fact that in Christ you are dead to sin and its power. Thinking this way equips you to resist temptation so that you 'do not let sin reign in your mortal body'. Neither will you have a desire to offer 'parts of your body to sin'.

Think God's thoughts and you will live God's way more effectively. Think like Christ; become like Christ.

6. Feed Your Mind

God's mind and will are perfectly revealed in his Word, the Bible. There is not a single issue in life into which his Word does not speak. As you fill your mind full of that Word, you will begin to see each situation you encounter through God's eyes and react to it as he would. Knowing God's Word will change your life, not in the sense of a learning exercise but by knowing it in your mind and heart - then putting it into practice:

'Do not merely listen to the word, and so deceive yourselves. Do what it says.'
(James 1:22) (See also Matthew 7:24-27.)

One function of the Holy Spirit is to remind us of God's Word and his ways as we find ourselves in the many and varied situations of life. Jesus promised that:

'The Holy Spirit, whom the Father will send in my name, will teach you all things and will remind you of everything I have said to you.'
(John 14:26)

We can only be reminded of what we have once heard or known. It is therefore our responsibility to feed our minds with God's Word so that the Spirit has a resource to work with as he guides us 'into all truth' (John 16:13).

7. Think it - Become it

You will change as you start to think in line with God's Word. **You will:**

a. Know God's will

'Be transformed by the renewing of your mind. Then you will be able to test and approve what God's will is - his good, pleasing and perfect will.'
(Romans 12:2)

b. Live free from sin

'How can a young man keep his way pure? By living according to your word... I have hidden your word in my heart that I might not sin against you.'
(Psalm 119:9, 11)

c. Be thoroughly equipped

'All scripture is God-breathed and is useful for teaching, rebuking, correcting and training in righteousness, so that the man of God may be thoroughly equipped for every good work.'
(2 Timothy 3:16-17)

8. Conclusion

'As [a man] thinks within himself , so he is .'
(Proverbs 23:7 NIV margin)

How you are today is a direct result of how you have thought up to this point in time. What you feel and experience now has been conditioned by what you have let your mind dwell upon, even today.

The sort of person you will be in the future depends on how you think from this point onwards. Make a conscious decision to work with God by filling your mind with his thoughts so that it can be your boast that:

'We will have confidence on the day of judgment, because in this world we are like [Christ].'
(1 John 4:17)

Lesson 1

Group Discussion Questions

1. Discuss biblical examples of people whose lives reflected the particular way they thought.

2. Each person share from his or her own experience an example of how, as they have thought within themselves, so they have become.

3. What place does our thought life play in the 'working out' of our salvation?

Personal Application

1. Prayerfully make an honest assessment of the way you think and how it affects your life in the following areas:

■ Your attitudes to other people

■ Your general outlook on life

■ Your speech

■ Your behaviour

■ Your character development

2. Memorise Romans 12:2.

3. Determine to stop conforming to this world's pattern, to renew your mind with God's Word and to live it out. Thank God that you know you are going to become more like Christ as you do this.

NOTES

Lesson 2

UNDERSTANDING THE BATTLE

We saw in lesson 1 that what controls our mind in effect controls our whole being. Understanding this important principle helps us to see why we sometimes feel that our mind is a battlefield. Conflicting thoughts, attitudes, hopes, fears and aspirations seek to dominate our mind and, consequently, our whole being.

1. The Battle is Spiritual

As Christians we must first recognise that the mental battle we sometimes experience is essentially a spiritual conflict.

Winning the battle is not simply a matter of 'mental gymnastics' or 'the power of positive thinking'. It is waging a spiritual warfare against Satan, who is seeking to bring confusion, doubt and fear into our minds. His aim is to lock us up and make us ineffective in our Christian living.

'Our struggle is not against flesh and blood, but against the rulers, against the authorities, against the powers of this dark world and against the spiritual forces of evil in the heavenly realms.'
(Ephesians 6:12)

2. Know Your Position

The battle for the mind is not a conflict between spiritual armies seeking to dominate the empty ground of your mind. It is not a struggle between evil thoughts which seek to enter your mind from one side and godly thoughts trying to gain access from the other - as often depicted in cartoons which show an angel sitting on one of your shoulders and a devil on the other, both making conflicting suggestions to you! This is not a battle for possession of your mind.

Why? Because your mind is already under a controlling influence; the ground of your mind is already Christ's. The Bible teaches that:

'We have the mind of Christ.'
(1 Corinthians 2:16)

The battle for your mind is therefore waged from a place of possession. It is a battle to hold the ground of our mind for Christ. This conflict is more about standing your ground and defending your position in Christ from any thought that tries to dislodge you.

'Put on the full armour of God so that you can take your stand against the devil's schemes... Therefore put on the full armour of God, so that when the day of evil comes, you may be able to stand your ground, and after you have done everything, to stand.'
(Ephesians 6:11, 13)

3. Know Who You Are

In Christ we have won our ground. Satan schemes to depose us but he is destined to fail as we stand firm in the sure knowledge of who we are in Christ. We know with certainty that:

'His divine power has given us everything we need for life and godliness through our knowledge of him.'
(2 Peter 1:3)

'Greater is he who is in you than he who is in the world.'
(1 John 4:4 NASB)

The more you get to know who you are in Christ, what you have available to you by being in Christ and all that you can do because you are in Christ, the easier it will be to win the battle for your mind.

4. Know Your Weapons

Knowing who you are in Christ is therefore part of your weaponry in the battle. Paul developed this thought a bit further in his letter to the church at Ephesus where he practically applied this principle to actual pieces of armour. Each piece must be in place to ensure we are fully protected and ready for battle:

a. Truth

'Stand firm then, with the belt of truth buckled round your waist.'
(Ephesians 6:14)

Jesus also said:

'If you hold to my teaching, you are really my disciples. Then you will know the truth, and the truth will set you free.'
(John 8:31-32)

Your mind needs to be filled with the truth of God's Word; truth about how God sees you and your situation, truth about God's ability and truth about your enemy's limitations. Knowing the truth about these things will set you free from mental turmoil.

b. Righteousness

'Stand firm... with the breastplate of righteousness in place.'
(Ephesians 6:14)

The moment you were saved, you received the gift of righteousness. You were made clean in Christ and have been declared to be holy by the judge in the courtroom of heaven! Knowing you are fundamentally righteous and therefore overwhelmingly right as you make choices and do things God's way, releases you to reign in life:

'How much more will those who receive God's abundant provision of grace and of the gift of righteousness reign in life through the one man, Jesus Christ.'
(Romans 5:17)

God's righteous ways are revealed fully in his Word, which tells us how to act or react in every situation of life. So, fill your mind with God's righteous Word - it is part of your armour!

c. The gospel

'Stand firm... with your feet fitted with the readiness that comes from the gospel of peace.'
(Ephesians 6:14-15)

A readiness to share the good news of salvation with people you meet demands a prepared mind, one filled with the blessings of being in Christ. By dwelling on these blessings we arm ourselves to repel any thought which suggests that life is better outside of Christ.

d. Faith

'Take up the shield of faith, with which you can extinguish all the flaming arrows of the evil one.'
(Ephesians 6:16)

Faith comes by hearing 'the word of Christ' (Romans 10:17). Fill your mind with who God says you are in Christ, have in Christ and can do in Christ. This will produce a faith in you that can repel anything Satan may throw at you and one which will keep you in victory.

'This is the victory that has overcome the world, even our faith.'
(1 John 5:4)

e. The hope of salvation

'Since we belong to the day, let us be self-controlled, putting on faith and love as a breastplate, and the hope of salvation as a helmet.'
(1 Thessalonians 5:8)

The helmet protects the head. Our minds should therefore be protected by a knowledge of our glorious hope in Christ.

'I pray... that the eyes of your heart may be enlightened in order that you may know the hope to which he has called you.'
(Ephesians 1:18)

Hope in this context is not some vague wish. A more literal translation would be 'confident expectation'. In other words, what God has said will certainly happen. Fill your mind with the certainty of God's promises to you and the assurance that you will be with him forever.

f. The Word of God

'Take the... sword of the Spirit, which is the word of God.'
(Ephesians 6:17)

Truth, righteousness, faith, the gospel and our hope of salvation are all described above as pieces of protective armour - yet they all have their roots in the Word of God, which is an offensive weapon. We wield the Word of God as a sword which cuts through Satan's lies and deceptions and helps us to stand firm in all that God has made us.

Your knowledge of God's Word is the mightiest weapon you have in fighting the battle for your mind. Therefore:

'Let the word of Christ dwell in you richly.'
(Colossians 3:16)

5. The Battle Defined

Based on what we have seen so far we can now define with some understanding the battle that takes place in our mind:

The Battle for the Mind is: ***a conflict between what you know you are in Christ, based on the Word of God, and any thought which undercuts, minimises or denies that truth.***

Satan seeks to use every means available to win this battle. He stirs up old thought patterns, feelings and reactions from our life before we came to Christ in an effort to make us a prisoner to them again. Paul observed that:

'I find this law at work: When I want to do good, evil is right there with me. For in my inner being I delight in God's law; but I see another law at work in the members of my body, waging war against the law of my mind and making me a prisoner of the law of sin at work within my members... So then, I myself in my mind am a slave to God's law, but in the sinful nature a slave to the law of sin.'
(Romans 7:21-23, 25)

The mind of Christ in Paul is engaged in a war with his old fleshly appetites. He knows that if he lets Satan use them to fill his mind he will again be a prisoner to sin.

When we let wrong thinking have a foothold in our mind it binds us and nullifies our effectiveness for Christ.

'Do not give the devil a foothold.'
(Ephesians 4:27)

An awareness of this should make us determined to declare, like Paul: 'I myself in my mind am a slave to God's law' (Romans 7:25).

6. The Form the Battle Takes

In our daily lives we can at any time find ourselves with a battle in our minds. Although we have a knowledge of who we are in Christ and a genuine desire to live God's way, any given situation can throw into our mind thoughts which undercut or deny the truth of all that we know. That becomes the *point of conflict*.

Sometimes these thoughts are a *response* to a particular situation we find ourselves in. For example, we see something or meet someone which triggers a memory and that thought throws us into mental turmoil. At other times they just seem to arrive in our minds out of the blue and we have no idea where they came from, they are *random* thoughts. Whatever their source or reason for being there, we must train our minds to respond to them in all of life's situations from the solid base of God's Word and not with anything which Satan may try to insert in its place.

Here are some examples how *random* and *response* thoughts can produce a battle in our mind:

a. Negative thoughts

The Situation:

A few days before you and your family are due to go on vacation a note arrives home with your child from school to say that there is an outbreak of chicken-pox. It asks that you therefore take care that as soon as you suspect your child has been in contact with the disease, he is kept off school.

The Battle:

Satan's response thought:

'So much for your holiday ... It's probably in his system already ... Chicken-pox in sunny Spain will be fun! ... Cancel it now and buy some calamine lotion.'

God's response thought:

'God's Word tells me: "The Lord will keep you free from every disease" (Deuteronomy 7:15) ... I know that "by his wounds I have been healed" (1 Peter 2:24) ... So we don't expect to get it.'

b. Memories of past failures

The Situation:

You are serving in a church context helping a group of new Christians get to grips with their new faith. You love serving them practically and happily make the drinks and chat informally to them. Then the leader approaches you over coffee and suggests that once the cups are cleared you come and share with the group how you became a Christian... and you are in the battle! On one hand you'd love to but on the other, you have been here before:

The Battle:

Satan's response thought:

'Remember the last time? ... You got your words mixed up and looked a real idiot! ... Keep quiet and preserve your self-respect.'

God's response thought:

'I need to share my testimony for everyone's benefit ... God says that people sharing his word do so "for their strengthening, encouragement and comfort" (1 Corinthians 14:3) ... I want these great people to be encouraged and God to be glorified, not me, so I'm going to share it.'

c. Fear

The Situation:

Before becoming a Christian you suffered from claustrophobia (fear of enclosed spaces) but have known a real release from its grip. Then one day while shopping you are in a crowded lift which suddenly breaks down! The battle is on:

The Battle:

Satan's response thought:

'I don't like this ... I may never get out ... I can't breathe ... I'm going to scream.'

God's response thought:

'I don't like this ... Once I would have panicked ... But Praise God, his perfect love for me has removed my fear (1 John 4:18).'

d. Sudden temptation

On other occasions the battle is suddenly raging in your mind in the form of a temptation to do something that you know you shouldn't.

For example: You are stood in the middle of a Department Store waiting for your wife to pay for her things and keeping an eye on your children when into your mind drifts the thought: 'I could steal that.

Everything is so open and people are everywhere; no one would see.' A battle in your mind is suddenly raging between this satanic intrusion and your knowledge that to steal is sin.

Or maybe as a young man you walk into a newsagents to collect your magazine or paper. Your eye catches the 'girly' magazines on the top shelf and the thought is suddenly in your mind: 'Have a quick look.' Again this produces a mental battle between the passing satanic intrusion and your knowledge that it would be wrong to do so.

7. Prepared for Battle

The common factor in all the examples above is that the situations described brought the 'mind of Christ' within you into conflict with response thoughts from the enemy. The mind of Christ expressed by God's Word was also the common resource in dealing with the conflict.

You must be prepared for the battle because it can be on you at anytime and many times a day. But that need not be a problem; you can live in victory and win the battle every time as we shall describe in our next lesson. That's because you *are not unaware of [Satan's] schemes' (2 Corinthians 2:10-11)* and have *'put on the full armour of God so that you can take your stand against the devil's schemes'* (Ephesians 6:11).

Satan may try to outwit us with his schemes - but we are ready for battle. Filled with the Word of God we are armed for battle and confident of victory, knowing that:

'The one who is in you is greater than the one who is in the world.' (1 John 4:4)

Lesson 2

Group Discussion Questions

1. Discuss why it is important that we understand that the battle for the mind is a spiritual one?

2. Each member of the group share one aspect of who they are in Christ. Did Satan try to tell you differently? How did you win the battle?

3. What resources do we have at our disposal in the battle for the mind?

Personal Application

1. Prayerfully make a list of the things about which you find greatest conflict in your mind. With the help of a concordance and/or Christian friend find out what God has to say about each issue.

2. Memorise 1 John 4:4.

3. Meditate upon Ephesians 6:10-17 and apply each piece of armour to the way you think - section four of this lesson will help you do this.

NOTES

Lesson 3

TAKING YOUR
THOUGHTS CAPTIVE

We established in lesson 1 that as a person 'thinks within himself, so he is' (Proverbs 23:7). It is of great importance how we think and what we think about because this will play a central role in the formation of our character, personality and behaviour patterns. Recognising this principle then also makes it more important than ever that we win the Battle for the Mind, as we described it in the previous lesson. So, let's get practical!

In this lesson we will look at just how we can control our thoughts on a daily basis. Don't forget, we are not at the mercy of every passing thought that drifts into our minds - we have the ability to take each one captive and control it:

'We demolish arguments and every pretension that sets itself up against the knowledge of God, and we take captive every thought to make it obedient to Christ.'
(2 Corinthians 10:4-5)

1. Creatures of Choice

In his wisdom God created man with a free will. We are creatures of choice able within certain bounds to determine our own success or failure in life.

Our coming into a relationship with God was an issue of choice. Though we now know that God *'chose us in [Christ] before the creation of the world' (Ephesians 1:4)*, at the point of our salvation it was our choice, an act of our free will, to open the door of our heart and invite Christ in:

'Here I am! I stand at the door and knock. If anyone hears my voice and opens the door, I will come in and eat with him, and he with me.'
(Revelation 3:20)

In our ongoing Christian life we are confronted with issues of choice on a daily basis. We should determine in our hearts to follow Christ wholeheartedly by deliberately choosing to live in the centre of his will at all times. Like Joshua, our attitude to God's word and ways should be:

'Choose for yourselves this day whom you will serve ... But as for me and my household, we will serve the Lord.'
(Joshua 24:15)

In fact, sometimes we do not have the things God wants for us simply because we do not choose to ask him for them. God loves to respond to the prayers of his people when those requests come from a pure heart of love for God and a desire to outwork his purpose for our lives:

'Ask and it will be given to you; seek and you will find; knock and the door will be opened to you. For everyone who asks receives; he who seeks finds; and to him who knocks, the door will be opened.'
(Matthew 7:7-8)

'You do not have, because you do not ask God.'
(James 4:2)

This ability to exercise free will and choice extends into the area of thought and mind control. You can choose what to think about and therefore affect the type of person you will ultimately become.

2. Worked In and Worked Out

At the point of our salvation God started a life-embracing work in each of us. We were reborn and made new creations so that the old was replaced with the new (2 Corinthians 5:17). Our responsibility now is to work out what he has worked into us.

'Continue to work out your salvation with fear and trembling, for it is God who works in you to will and to act according to his good purpose.'
(Philippians 2:12-13)

As you grow in your understanding of what God has done for you in salvation, you must choose to work it out. You decide whether or not to do his will in all and every situation you ever face in life.

3. God's Incentives

If you think about it, your decision to give your life to Christ was prompted by both a positive and a negative incentive:

'The wages of sin is death, but the gift of God is eternal life in Christ Jesus our Lord.'
(Romans 6:23)

So, on one hand you were motivated by a desire to avoid the consequences of your sin and on the other by a desire to possess the eternal life Jesus offered. These two incentives continue to be involved in every subsequent choice you make as a Christian - not in the ultimate sense of gaining or losing your salvation - but as a check and balance to ensure you make right choices in accordance with God's Word and ways. New believers soon learn that God blesses those who obey him wholeheartedly and withdraws his favour from those who disobey his Word and walk in sin. The Old Testament puts it this way:

'If you fully obey the Lord your God and carefully follow all his commands that I give you today, the Lord your God will set you high above all the nations on earth. All these blessings will come upon you and accompany you if you obey the Lord your God ... However, if you do not obey the Lord your God and do not carefully follow all his commands and decrees I am giving you today, all these curses will come upon you and overtake you.'
(Deuteronomy 28:1-2, 15)

Now transfer this to the realm of your mind because every decision to obey or disobey starts there. Every choice to think about something in particular will lead you on a path to either favour and blessing or draw you away from God. In fact the Bible teaches that we will have to give an account to God for every thought we think, word we speak and deed we do. This truth provokes us to live in a healthy fear of God! We deliberately think in line with God's will and deal with any sinful thoughts which would cause us to live contrary to his desire for us. As wise Solomon noted:

'Through the fear of the Lord a man avoids evil.'
(Proverbs 16:6)

'The fear of the Lord leads to life: Then one rests content, untouched by trouble.'
(Proverbs 19:23)

4. You Are in Control

Many people who are locked into wrong patterns of living recognise that the way they think is part of the problem. But their defence for not changing their thoughts and behaviour is usually: 'I just can't help thinking these things. I know they're wrong but they just keep coming back into my mind.' I'm sure we can all identify with that sort of comment but it is the thin end of a large wedge of deception. It is a statement of helplessness and a complete abdication of responsibility. It is the beginning of 'blame shifting' whether it is to Satan, your past, a particular person or whatever. And it is wrong! Satan certainly is the source of some sinful thoughts, as are your past experiences, memories and the things you see or hear, but that does not absolve you from the responsibility of handling them correctly when they arrive in your mind.

Consider the following scriptures, noting particularly what we are required to do for ourselves:

'We take captive every thought to make it obedient to Christ.'
(2 Corinthians 10:5)

'You were taught, with regard to your former way of life, to put off your old self, which is being corrupted by its deceitful desires; to be made new in the attitude of your minds; and to put on the new self, created to be like God in true righteousness and holiness.'
(Ephesians 4:22-24)

'Set your minds on things above, not on earthly things'
(Colossians 3:2)

'Whatever is true, whatever is noble, whatever is right, whatever is pure, whatever is lovely, whatever is admirable - if anything is excellent or praiseworthy - think about such things.'
(Philippians 4:8)

How could God give us commands like these if it was impossible for us to do it? It would be unjust of him. No, our responsibility is to 'take captive', 'put off', 'put on' and deliberately 'think about' - in other words, let our minds dwell only on wholesome thoughts. We must literally sift our thoughts and entertain only those that will work for good in our lives.

Imagine for a moment that your mind is the air space over a major airport. Your thoughts are like the aircraft which constantly pass through that air space. You are the person in the control tower who has ultimate control of which aircraft are given permission to land on your territory. You allow aircraft from friendly nations to land. But if an enemy plane enters your air space and seeks permission to land, you have to make an important choice. Do you refuse and send your fighter planes up to chase him off? Or do you take a chance and let him land?

You must make a similar choice with every thought that enters the air space of your mind. Someone once said: 'No one would allow garbage at his table but many allow it to be served into their minds.' Take control, because you can! You have the ability to entertain and ultimately produce the fruit of every thought that enters your 'air space'. You are not at mercy of every passing thought - they are at yours!

5. Take and Make

Here's how to do it:

'We take captive every thought to make it obedient to Christ.'
(2 Corinthians 10:5)

The New Testament in Basic English renders this verse: 'Causing every thought to come under the authority of Christ.' In order to take hold of a thought, make it obedient to Christ's authority and then deal with it accordingly, we must have a rule or basis upon which to sort our thoughts out. This I call the 'thought filter'.

a. The thought filter

Because we want to be like Christ, we need to filter our thoughts in such a way that those which reflect his heart, mind and will are entertained, and those which are clearly contrary to his will are rejected. Our criteria for doing this is a knowledge of what God *approves* and what he *hates*. Knowing this gives us a firm basis on which to sort every thought entering our mind.

Your knowledge of what God hates and approves is so fundamental to your success in the battle for your mind that Satan seeks to undermine it. He tries to argue against what you know to be the truth. Scripture provides the answer to this:

'We demolish arguments and every pretension that sets itself up against the knowledge of God.'
(2 Corinthians 10:5)

The battle is against every thought that sets itself against the knowledge of God (as stated in our definition of the 'Battle for the Mind' in Lesson 2).

Your knowledge of God and what he approves and hates will only be as great as two interacting factors:

● Your knowledge of God's Word.
● Your sensitivity to the Holy Spirit's promptings within you.

Together these constitute the 'thought filter'.

b. Using the filter

The Holy Spirit in you and your knowledge of God's Word equip you to deal with every wrong thought. Each thought is taken captive and filtered to find out:

● Does it agree with God's Word?
● Does it grieve or rest easily with the Holy Spirit within me (Ephesians 4:30)?

It is then handled accordingly.

An easy way to remember how to use the thought filter is by memorising three simple words:

❏ Recognise

Recognise the source of the thought by lining it up with your knowledge of God's Word and what the Spirit says to your heart. In other words, 'make it obedient to Christ'.

❏ Refuse

If its source is Satan or any other negative source, refuse to dwell on it. Actively put the thought out of your mind. Refuse to conform to it. Do what Paul told the Romans: *'Do not conform any longer to the pattern of this world, but be transformed by the renewing of your mind.'* *(Romans 12:2)*

If necessary speak out loud to the thought or whatever you perceive the source of the thought to be. Strongly resist this intrusion into your mind, confident that as you *'Submit yourselves to God, resist the devil and he will flee from you.' (James 4:7)*

❏ Replace

Thirdly, and most importantly, replace the negative, evil, critical or impure thoughts with God's Word. Most Christians are good at the first two steps but struggle when the thought they try and push from their mind keeps reappearing as if on elastic! They key is not to leave your mind empty. Once you have recognised and refused a bad thought you *must* replace it with something greater than and opposite to it. This is where your knowledge of God's Word becomes vital.

'I meditate on your precepts and consider your ways. I delight in your decrees; I will not neglect your word.'
(Psalm 119:15-16)

Replacing the wrong thought with a good one is vital so that it is not able to bounce straight back once you've refused it. Replace it by filling your mind with all God's goodness to you.

6. Filtered Thinking

Imagine that as you are walking along the cliff tops, the thought to throw yourself off suddenly comes into your mind:

❏ Recognise

It is from Satan, who seeks only to *'steal and kill and destroy'* *(John 10:10).*

❏ Refuse

Resolutely refuse it in Jesus' name. Speak out loud if necessary.

❏ Replace

Fill your mind with thoughts of God's promises to you; thoughts of the hope and future you have (Jeremiah 29:11); thoughts of your destiny and calling. Throwing yourself off the cliff soon becomes the silliest thing imaginable; you have a great life ahead! And if a tinge of fear touches your heart as the thought arrives remind yourself of God's love and protection; remember, *'The angel of the Lord encamps around those who fear him, and he delivers them.' (Psalm 34:7)*

Imagine that you are in a situation at work where your boss asks you to do something which you know is unrighteous. The thought comes: 'I'd better do it because, if I don't, I could lose my job.'

❏ Recognise

It is from Satan, who is the deceiver and the source of all unrighteousness.

❏ Refuse

Determine not to let fear of your employer, or fear of unemployment, stop you from doing what is right.

❏ Replace

Fill your mind with thoughts of how God honours and rewards people of integrity. His word says: *'The man of integrity walks securely' (Proverbs 10:9)* and that is what you are determined to be. Be careful, too, that you don't allow the fear of your boss to snare you. Scripture warns us about this but also gives us a great promise: *'The fear of man will prove to be a snare, but whoever trusts in the Lord is kept safe' (Proverbs 29:25)*. Each day walk into work saying to yourself: *'The Lord is with me; I will not be afraid. What can man do to me?' (Psalm 118:6)*

7. Guard the Gates

The more you understand the principle we are explaining in this study, the more you will realise that many of the wrong thought patterns that produced a battle in your mind could have been prevented simply by guarding the access points to your mind. Such thoughts are often the product of situations you knowingly walk into. By guarding the gates to your mind you can in many instances pre-empt Satan's efforts to intrude into your thinking.

If you keep your mind sufficiently open, people will throw a lot of rubbish into it. It comes at us from every angle and we must take responsibility for every access point to our mind, not just deal with the thoughts once they get there. Guarding the gates or access points to your mind includes:

a. Your Eyes

'The eye is the lamp of the body. If your eyes are good, your whole body will be full of light. But if your eyes are bad, your whole body will be full of darkness.'
(Matthew 6:22-23)

Guard what you look at. Many thoughts find access to your mind through what you see. The television programmes and DVDs you watch, the books and magazines you read, the films you go to see, can all be a springboard for positive or negative thinking. Some give Satan an opportunity to plant a range of evil, fearful or unclean thoughts in your mind. So instead, feed your mind with good things by reading the Scriptures and other helpful literature and by watching films, DVDs and films that are edifying as well as enjoyable. We need to guard what we look at as Job did. He said:

'I made a covenant with my eyes not to look lustfully at a girl.'
(Job 31:1)

b. Your Legs

Guard where you go. Many wrong thoughts are triggered off by our being in the wrong place. Remember David's sin with Bathsheba? This didn't take place just because he saw her. The truth is that he shouldn't have even been in the palace at that time:

'In the spring, at the time when kings go off to war, David sent Joab out with the king's men and the whole Israelite army.'
(2 Samuel 11:1)

David should have been out with his army but instead sent someone else and therefore had time to let his eyes and mind wander.

So the lesson is, if you know that attending certain parties or going to specific places will give Satan an opportunity to put wrong thoughts your way - don't let your legs take you there!

c. Your Company

Guard who you spend time with. It is a fact that we become like those with whom we spend our time. Recognising this, the Bible exhorts us:

'Do not make friends with a hot-tempered man, do not associate with one easily angered, or you may learn his ways and get yourself ensnared.'
(Proverbs 22:24-25)

'Bad company corrupts good character.'
(1 Corinthians 15:33)

This doesn't mean that we should never mix with non-Christians. It does, however, put a responsibility on us to choose our friends wisely. Worldly people will instil worldly values into us if we let them; godly people will provoke us to godliness.

'As iron sharpens iron, so one man sharpens another.'
(Proverbs 27:17)

d. Your Ears

Guard what you listen to. What we hear goes into our minds whether we like it or not, we then have to deal with it. In some situations, however, we can prevent ourselves from hearing potentially bad things by taking suitable precautions. For example, don't entertain gossip. If a person starts telling you some gossip about a third person, refuse to listen. In this way you prevent a seed of division entering your mind and becoming a barrier between you and the third person.

'A gossip betrays a confidence; so avoid a man who talks too much.'
(Proverbs 20:19)

Similarly, don't let negative words fill your mind with doubts and fears. If for example, watching the TV news late at night sends you to bed depressed and pessimistic about the future, watch it in the morning when you are mentally stronger and there are more positive people and things around to occupy your mind.

'You will guard him and keep him in perfect and constant peace whose mind (both its inclination and its character) is stayed on you.'
(Isaiah 26:3 Amplified)

e. Your Feelings

Guard your reaction to your moods and feelings.

'Whatever is true, whatever is noble, whatever is right, whatever is pure, whatever is lovely, whatever is admirable - if anything is excellent or praiseworthy - think about such things.'
(Philippians 4:8)

Our application of this verse does not depend upon how we feel. So often the 'Monday morning blues' or changing moods enable Satan to plant wrong thoughts in your mind. Instead, fill your mind with good things, however you feel. As you do this, declaring them to God and yourself, you will start to feel better too!

'Why are you downcast, O my soul? Why so disturbed within me? Put your hope in God, for I will yet praise him, my Saviour and my God.'
(Psalm 42:5-6)

8. Conclusion

Guard the gates to your mind. In this way you will immediately reduce the ability of the enemy to sow wrong thoughts into your mind.

Take captive and 'make obedient to Christ' any that do pass the gate. Thus you will fill your mind only with God's thoughts and serve to speed the transformation of your whole being into the image and likeness of Christ (2 Corinthians 3:18).

LESSON 3

Group Discussion Questions

1. How do God's incentives help us choose to live and think his way?

2. How do we handle recurring wrong thoughts?

3. Discuss the effect that people around us can have on our ability to take our thoughts captive.

Personal Application

1. Memorise 2 Corinthians 10:5.

2. Identify particular areas where you struggle regularly with wrong thoughts. Apply the 'thought filter' to these areas by memorising suitable scriptures with which to replace the wrong thoughts.

3. Prayerfully consider why the conflict in your mind occurs. Are you guarding the gates of your mind? Be prepared to make radical changes in your lifestyle if necessary.

NOTES

Lesson 4
DEVELOPING A FAITH IMAGE

'To him who is able to do immeasurably more than all we ask or imagine, according to his power that is at work within us, to him be glory in the church and in Christ Jesus throughout all generations, for ever and ever! Amen.'
(Ephesians 3:20-21)

Having seen how important the way we think is, we will now consider how we can develop a positive Bible-based vision for every aspect of our individual lives. This vision will also equip us to succeed in the battles of the mind. We will call this our *faith image*.

1. What is a Faith Image?

Faith is described in Hebrews 11:1 as *'being sure of what we hope for and certain of what we do not see'*. It is the firm persuasion and expectation that God will perform all that he has promised us in Christ. The certainty of faith rests in the fact that it is based on the unchanging Word of God (Romans 10:17).

An **image** is defined as a 'mental representation; idea, conception'. It is something I imagine - a picture, vision or thought in my mind.

My **faith image** can therefore be defined as:

What I am certain I will become in Christ, based on the unchanging Word of God.

55

In the natural world dreams are powerful. Martin Luther King motivated millions through his famous 'I have a dream' speech. Another wise observer said: 'The most has come to those with the greatest dreams.' And it's true. Without a vision or goal, man is not motivated to achieve his full potential in life.

If this is true in the natural realm, how much more it is in the spiritual, where our vision and goals - our faith image - is not based simply on our own good ideas, but on what God says we can become. Our faith image is based solidly on God's Word and comes into being through the working of his power within us:

'[God] is able to do immeasurably more than all we ask or imagine, according to his power that is at work within us.'
(Ephesians 3:20)

Unless we come to terms with the powerful resource we have in Christ, we will never 'ask or imagine' much outside our natural ability. It takes a revelation of God's greatness to motivate you to dream beyond your natural abilities. Knowing this, Paul writes to the Ephesians:

'I pray ... that the eyes of your heart may be enlightened in order that you may know the hope to which he has called you, the riches of his glorious inheritance in the saints, and his incomparably great power for us who believe. That power is like the working of his mighty strength, which he exerted in Christ when he raised him from the dead.'
(Ephesians 1:18-20)

Conscious of his resources in Christ, Paul had a faith image for himself and those with whom he laboured. He knew he could attain his goal; he knew he could bring men to maturity (Colossians 1:28) because his faith image encapsulated the heart of God for both himself and his fellow-workers:

'One thing I do: Forgetting what is behind and straining towards what is ahead, I press on towards the goal to win the prize for which God has called me heavenwards in Christ Jesus.'
(Philippians 3:13-14)

2. The Complete You

Your faith image should encapsulate what God wants you to become. As Christians we need to release our God-filled imaginations to see what God can and will accomplish in and through us before we die. Someone once said: 'Many aspire, few attain.' In Christ this is not necessarily true. If your aspiration is based in God's will and purpose for you, you will attain it.

In the scripture below we read of a woman who had a faith image of herself being made well:

'A woman who had been subject to bleeding for twelve years came up behind him and touched the edge of his cloak. She said to herself, "If I only touch his cloak, I will be healed." Jesus turned and saw her. "Take heart, daughter," he said, "your faith has healed you." And the woman was healed from that moment.'
(Matthew 9:20-22)

In her mind's eye she saw herself back to normal, completely whole. She knew that if she touched Jesus she would recover. That was her faith image - it was what she was certain she would become.

What does God say about you? Does he want to finish something in you? Yes! God's desire is to transform you into a person who truly represents the full glory of Christ's character - in this life.

'He who began a good work in you will carry it on to completion until the day of Christ Jesus.'
(Philippians 1:6)

3. See it - Become it

We must have a revelation of what God wants to accomplish in us before we can accomplish it. You must see what you can become before you can become what you see.

This is the essence of a faith image. See yourself complete in Christ and you are then motivated to move towards it.

'Perseverance must finish its work so that you may be mature and complete, not lacking anything.'
(James 1:4)

'... until we all reach unity in the faith and in the knowledge of the Son of God and become mature, attaining to the whole measure of the fullness of Christ'.
(Ephesians 4:13)

Ask God to give you a revelation of his fullness. Fill your mind and heart with this faith image. You will then start to become what you have asked and imagined - and more (Ephesians 3:20)!

4. Be What You Are

Your faith image is not an unattainable goal. As you cease to conform to the pattern of this world and fill your mind with God's purpose for you, you will achieve it (Romans 12:2). You are, in fact, becoming what you *already are*. You have within you the full potential to develop a mellow Christlike character in this life.

Scripture teaches that our spiritual rebirth can be likened to a natural birth in which a single microscopic sperm carries all the father's characteristics into the newborn baby. As the child grows, these traits become seen in its character and appearance.

'You have been born again, not of perishable seed, but of imperishable, through the living and enduring word of God.'
(1 Peter 1:23)

At your spiritual birth a 'seed' was deposited within you. The word 'seed' used in the above text is the Greek word 'sperma' from which we derive our word sperm. At spiritual rebirth the seed of our heavenly Father was deposited within us. That seed carries all his character qualities and as we grow spiritually they become more and more evident in the form of a Christlike character.

You can become what you already are in seed form. Release your mind to consider the fullness of what you have become in Christ. Think in line with this faith image of yourself, act upon it - and you will start to become it.

5. A Sober Start

It is important that, in developing and working towards your faith image, you start from the right place. This should be the condition you find yourself in right now. If you want to run a marathon, your training starts with a sober assessment of your present fitness. If you are totally unfit you don't plan to run fifteen miles each day in the first week! If, on the other hand, you know that you can manage three miles quite easily, you can work up from this point to the full twenty-six miles over a period of time.

You may have a faith image - but your first step to taking possession of it is to know your current spiritual condition. You can then work towards it from a right starting place.

a. Soberly assess your measure of faith

'By the grace given me I say to every one of you: Do not think of yourself more highly than you ought, but rather think of yourself with sober judgment, in accordance with the measure of faith God has given you.'
(Romans 12:3)

We are all in the 'school of faith' and growing as we take steps in full reliance on God's unchanging Word. Maybe you are growing in faith for health, finance, protection, wisdom, or some other aspect of life. Whatever it is, consider: What can you believe God for right now? As you use the faith you already have, it will grow until ultimately you will by faith be able to take hold of and become the 'fullness of Christ' (Ephesians 4:13).

b. Soberly assess your gift areas

'We have different gifts, according to the grace given us.'
(Romans 12:6)

What are you good at? What do you enjoy doing? Your faith image will embrace a development of your particular God-given gifts, skills and abilities. Get to know what they are so that you can develop them and not be sidetracked into a desire to be something you are not gifted at.

c. Soberly assess your present activity

'If anyone thinks he is something when he is nothing, he deceives himself. Each one should test his own actions. Then he can take pride in himself, without comparing himself to somebody else.'
(Galatians 6:3-4)

Work from your current activity towards your faith image. Are you doing things that are conducive to attaining your goal?

A young man I know had just returned from an overseas missions conference. He was really 'fired up' with enthusiasm and went to see one of his pastors to announce that God had called him to full-time missions work and he was therefore thinking of giving in his notice at work. He was met with something less than an enthusiastic response which deflated him. The pastor's observation was that up to this point he had shown no personal initiative in reaching the lost whatsoever, neither had he ever had any involvement with the church's various mission and outreach programmes. So, wasn't leaving work a bit premature? He had to be brought back into reality. His faith image was good but he was not starting from the right place. He had to see that he would only reach his goal if he took stock of where he was now and then took appropriate steps in the right direction.

What are you doing for God now? That is your sober starting place.

'Let every person carefully scrutinise and examine and test his own conduct and his own work.'
(Galatians 6.4 Amplified)

6. Feed Your Faith Image

Having taken stock and established a sober starting point, you now need to press on towards your faith image. Develop a strategy that causes your faith to grow, your gifts to develop and your activity to be channelled into purposeful tasks. The key to doing this is to feed your faith image.

'Faith comes from hearing the message, and the message is heard through the word of Christ.'
(Romans 10:17)

Because faith comes by hearing God's Word, we need to feed our dreams and thinking with scripture. Your faith image will then grow and develop as you come to understand more of God's ultimate purpose for you. Big ideas may feed your ego but they will do nothing for your faith - only God's word can cause faith to come in ever increasing measure.

Look into the Bible and see what it says about you. Start by asking the following three questions. A few examples are given in each instance.

a. What does God say I am?

'If anyone is in Christ, he is a new creation.'
(2 Corinthians 5:17)

'The Spirit himself testifies with our spirit that we are God's children.'
(Romans 8:16)

'In all these things we are more than conquerors.'
(Romans 8:37)

b. What does God say I can do?

'I can do everything through him who gives me strength.'
(Philippians 4:13)

'Apart from me you can do nothing.'
(John 15:5)

c. What does God say I have?

'God will meet all your needs according to his glorious riches in Christ Jesus.'
(Philippians 4:19)

'His divine power has given us everything we need for life and godliness.'
(2 Peter 1:3)

As you feed your mind with these truths about yourself, your faith image will develop and become established. You will be more certain than ever about what you are going to become in Christ.

7. Motivated to Succeed

'If at first you don't succeed... find a way to' was the slogan of one well known, very successful businessman. He was determined to find a way to succeed. For people like him, motivation and determination are key factors. We, too, must be motivated to succeed in our Christian life. This motivation comes from our faith image.

Even Jesus had a faith image. He knew with absolute certainty what the future held for him:

'Jesus knew that the Father had put all things under his power, and that he had come from God and was returning to God.'
(John 13:3)

Secure in this knowledge he was able to wash his disciples' feet, cleanse the Temple with a whip, expose the hypocrisy of the Pharisees - and even endure the cross. It didn't matter to him what people thought or whether the task was regarded as noble or servile in human terms. He did only his Father's will and was motivated to fulfil his task on earth by the certainty of future joy.

'Let us fix our eyes on Jesus, the author and perfecter of our faith, who for the joy set before him endured the cross, scorning its shame, and sat down at the right hand of the throne of God.'
(Hebrews 12:2)

That joy was the leading of many sons to glory and the sharing of his kingship with the redeemed people, his church.

Your faith image will produce in you a similar sense of destiny and motivate you to succeed in this life. It will even cause you to endure hardship and opposition, just like Christ did.

'Consider him who endured such opposition from sinful men, so that you will not grow weary and lose heart.'
(Hebrews 12:3)

It will also make you secure and confident in all you do for Christ, for you know that your faith image is from God and will be realised.

'Let us hold unswervingly to the hope we profess, for he who promised is faithful.'
(Hebrews 10:23)

8. And More . . .

Start developing a faith image. Fill your mind with God's glorious purpose for your life and start to work towards it, remembering that God *'is able to do immeasurably more than all we ask or imagine'* *(Ephesians 3:20)*.

LESSON 4

Group Discussion Questions

1. What is the difference between your 'faith image' and other things you may naturally aspire to?

2. Discuss together some aspects of God's purpose for you as an individual Christian.

3. Each person share (with Bible reference if possible) one thing God says that you are in Christ, you have in Christ and you can do in Christ.

Personal Application

Prayerfully develop a faith image:

1. Start by soberly assessing yourself, applying the points in section 5 of this lesson.

2. Ask God to reveal to you in the days ahead more of his purpose for your life. What kind of person has God destined you to be?

3. Discover what the Bible says about each area of your life and start to develop a faith image for it. The list below will start you on your way, though the scriptures given are not exhaustive.

God's will for you as:

a. A husband   Ephesians 5:25-33; Colossians 3:19; 1 Peter 3:7

b. A wife   Ephesians 5:22-24; Colossians 3:18; 1 Peter 3:1-6

c. A parent   Ephesians 6:4; Colossians 3:21

d. A child   Ephesians 6:1-3; Colossians 3:20

e. An employer   Ephesians 6:9; Colossians 4:1

f. An employee   Ephesians 6:5-8; Colossians 3:22-25

g. A citizen   Romans 13:1-7; 1 Timothy 2:1-4; 1 Peter 2:13-15

h. A church leader   Acts 20:28; 1 Peter 5:1-3

i. A church member Hebrews 13:17; 1 Thessalonians 5:12-13

4. Thank God for the greatness of his purpose for your life and start to move into it - and more!

NOTES

Lesson 5

MAINTAINING YOUR FAITH IMAGE

'He who began a good work in you will carry it on to completion until the day of Christ Jesus.'
(Philippians 1:6)

The passage of time affects different people in different ways. To some people time is a healer while to others it is a source of frustration. Still others reminisce on the events of past years, either with joy or sorrow. There is, however, one consequence of the passage of time to which we are all subject - we forget! Memories dim and past joys fade. What happens to God's Word in all this? Does that also fade? It must not if we are to reach our faith image.

1. 'Do Not Forget . . .'

Forgetfulness was one of the greatest enemies of God's people Israel. Only a short time after being miraculously delivered from Egypt, the people of Israel cry:

'It would have been better for us to serve the Egyptians than to die in the desert!'
(Exodus 14:12)

God intervenes and they are delivered through the parting of the Red Sea. Great rejoicing prevails for a time. Mighty miracles are wrought by God on their behalf, yet within eleven weeks:

'The whole community grumbled against Moses and Aaron. The Israelites said to them, "If only we had died by the Lord's hand in Egypt!"'
(Exodus 16:2-3)

We could illustrate this further, tracing the ups and downs of Israel's history. When they remembered what God had done for them and lived in the good of it, they were blessed and found success. When they forgot the Lord they fell into spiritual, social and moral decline. Consequently, God kept urging them to remember him:

*'Be careful, and watch yourselves closely so that you **do not forget** the things your eyes have seen or let them slip from your heart as long as you live. Teach them to your children and to their children after them.'*
(Deuteronomy 4:9)

The sad truth was that the many commands to remember the Lord were also forgotten and we eventually read:

'After that whole generation had been gathered to their fathers, another generation grew up, who knew neither the Lord nor what he had done for Israel. Then the Israelites did evil in the eyes of the Lord and served the Baals.'
(Judges 2:10-11)

2. Us Too!

Being prone to forget was not unique to the children of Israel; it is a trait of all humanity. No doubt God has spoken a clear word to you in a Sunday meeting and in the emotion of the occasion you have determined to put it into action straight away. After leaving the meeting you embark on your busy schedule. Suddenly, it is Tuesday lunchtime and you remember your commitment . . . !

Do you remember your initial zeal for Christ and how you were going to turn the world upside-down for him? Can you remember the excitement of stepping out in specific faith for the first time? Do you recall the impact that being baptised in the Holy Spirit had on you? Because God knows what we are like, the Bible is full of injunctions to remember him and his Word. Take the words of Isaiah for example, spoken at a time when Israel had rebelled against God:

'Remember this, fix it in mind, take it to heart, you rebels. Remember the former things, those of long ago; I am God, and there is no other; I am God, and there is none like me.'
(Isaiah 46:8-9)

In a similar way, the apostle John urged the church at Ephesus to remember their former zeal:

'I hold this against you: You have forsaken your first love. Remember the height from which you have fallen! Repent and do the things you did at first.'
(Revelation 2:4-5)

3. Stay Motivated

In the last lesson we saw how to develop a faith image - a Bible-based image of *what you are certain you will become in Christ*. If you have taken the appropriate steps, you have embarked on a clear course towards reaching your goal, motivated by the truths of God's Word. You must now stay motivated. You must maintain that initial enthusiasm and hold on to it through all of life's varied circumstances, proving God's Word and receiving its fulfilment in due time.

'We do not want you to become lazy, but to imitate those who through faith and patience inherit what has been promised.'
(Hebrews 6:12)

The word of faith that sped you on your way to fulfil God's purpose for your life must be outworked. For all of us it will mean patient endurance as we use God's Word to remind ourselves of the specifics about which God has spoken to us. We are confident of their ultimate fulfilment because:

'... my word that goes out from my mouth... will not return to me empty, but will accomplish what I desire and achieve the purpose for which I sent it.'
(Isaiah 55:11)

Don't let God's word to you fade from your mind but keep it uppermost. In this way you will maintain your faith image and press into it unperturbed by life's pressures.

4. The Test of Time

Abram had a faith image that stood the test of time. When he was seventy-five years old God gave him a promise that he would be the father of a great nation (Genesis 12:2). Yet he and Sarai were childless. God later confirmed his promise to Abram:

'He took him outside and said, "Look up at the heavens and count the stars - if indeed you can count them." Then he said to him, "So shall your offspring be." Abram believed the Lord, and he credited it to him as righteousness.'
(Genesis 15:5-6)

Abram believed God. Because God had spoken he knew he would one day have a son and heir. God then confirmed his covenant by changing his name from Abram ('exalted father') to Abraham ('father of many') (see 17:3-8).

In his mind he probably tried to imagine what his son and heir would be like. He pondered the things he would teach him and do with him, thus developing a faith image. Yet it was twenty-five years before Isaac was born (21:5). Abraham successfully maintained his faith image over this period by constantly remembering God's original word to him. It stood the test of time.

'He did not waver through unbelief regarding the promise of God, but was strengthened in his faith and gave glory to God, being fully persuaded that God had power to do what he had promised.'
(Romans 4:20-21)

5. Refresh Your Memory

'Faith comes from hearing the message, and the message is heard through the word of Christ.'
(Romans 10:17)

God's word to us is the source of our faith. Therefore, to maintain our faith image we need to keep that word fresh in our minds. Recognising the importance of this, the apostle Peter writes:

'I will always remind you of these things, even though you know them and are firmly established in the truth you now have. I think it is right to refresh your memory as long as I live in the tent of this body ... I will make every effort to see that after my departure you will always be able to remember these things.'
(2 Peter 1:12-13, 15)

Refresh your memory regularly. Meditate on God's great and precious promises to you. Then you will maintain your faith image.

The test of the genuineness of faith is seen when we encounter times of pressure or adverse circumstances which could take our mind and confidence away from God's word.

'These [trials] have come so that your faith - of greater worth than gold, which perishes even though refined by fire - may be proved genuine.'
(1 Peter 1:7)

At these times we truly discover that it is by faith and patience that we inherit the promise (Hebrews 6:12). Indeed, the testing of our faith in this way increases our capacity to persevere:

'because you know that the testing of your faith develops perseverance.'
(James 1:3)

In times of pressure refresh your memory like the psalmist who, when feeling low, remembered God's goodness:

'My soul is downcast within me; therefore I will remember you.'
(Psalm 42:6)

6. Keep it in Mind

The importance of keeping in mind God's word is graphically illustrated by the story of the men sent into Canaan to spy out the land. They all knew that it would be a land 'flowing with milk and honey' (Exodus 3:8). They had also all heard God speak about the way they would possess it:

'I will send my terror ahead of you and throw into confusion every nation you encounter. I will make all your enemies turn their backs and run.'
(Exodus 23:27)

All twelve spies knew what God had said. Why then was there a difference of opinion between Joshua and Caleb and the other ten spies about their ability to go in and possess the land (see Numbers 13:26-33; 14:6-9)? I believe the reason was that Joshua and Caleb always kept God's word in mind. They believed it and let it colour all they saw. So when they encountered the fortified cities and giants, they were not intimidated because they saw them with the eye of faith:

'Caleb silenced the people before Moses and said, "We should go up and take possession of the land, for we can certainly do it."'
(Numbers 13:30)

'Do not be afraid of the people of the land, because we will swallow them up. Their protection is gone, but the Lord is with us. Do not be afraid of them.'
(Numbers 14:9)

Joshua and Caleb had a faith image of Israel possessing the land as God had said.

Even though the other ten knew God's word, it was not filling their hearts and minds. Their memory was short and their confidence in God's word lacking. So when they saw the very same obstacles, they reasoned in their minds that the task was too great. They knew God's word but had not heard and received it in a way that would produce faith to overcome all obstacles. Hence they conclude:

'We can't attack those people; they are stronger than we are ... The land we explored devours those living in it. All the people we saw there are of great size ... We seemed like grasshoppers in our own eyes, and we looked the same to them.'
(Numbers 13:31-33)

An important key to maintaining your faith image is to have a memory refreshed by God's Word. Keep feeding your faith image. Then whenever difficulties seem to obstruct the path, through faith and patience you will overcome and inherit the promise.

'This is the victory that has overcome the world, even our faith.'
(1 John 5:4)

7. Stimulate Your Thinking

What is the first thing that comes into your mind when a problem arises in your life? Is it a cry of despair which leads to a horrible sinking feeling in your stomach? Is it a quick survey of your ability to handle the situation out of your own strengths? Or is it what God says about the situation?

We must train our minds to be so full of God's Word that we respond according to it in every situation. Just as an army trains continually in order to be ready for battle, our minds must be trained by God's Word so that we are always equipped to win the battle for the mind.

After Peter's exhortation to 'refresh your memory' (2 Peter 1:13), he gives the purpose of his letters:

'I have written both of them as reminders to stimulate you to wholesome thinking.'
(2 Peter 3:1)

His purpose was to make his readers think God's thoughts. He knew that this kind of wholesome thinking would lead to wholesome living. Notice in the next verse what he specifically requests them to do:

'I want you to recall the words spoken in the past by the holy prophets and the command given by our Lord and Saviour through your apostles.'
(2 Peter 3:2)

Peter urges us to recall, bring to mind and think about God's Word. And he mentions three sources of that Word: the prophets, Christ's commands and the apostles' teaching. This is what our minds should have on immediate recall to meet every situation life might bring. Sometimes it may seem a lot to remember:

'How precious to me are your thoughts, O God! How vast is the sum of them!'
(Psalm 139:17)

But, the more you get to know God's Word, the better equipped you will be to win the battles of your mind and maintain your faith image to its fulfilment. Before long, you won't have to ask: 'What does God say about this?' Instead, God's response will be in your mind and on your tongue automatically.

A Christian was once doing a crossword puzzle in his lunch break. One clue was simply 'Spirit' and the word had three letters. Discovering that the first letter was 'G', the Christian automatically entered 'GOD' (John 4:24). When he could go no further, his non-Christian colleague came to assist him and exclaimed. 'What on earth have you put GOD there for? It should be GIN!' Each answered from that which filled his mind! Stimulate your mind to think God's way.

8. Meditate on the Word

To meditate is to speak to yourself on the inside; to discuss and ponder inwardly over a matter. In order to maintain our faith image we need constantly to refresh our memories and stimulate our thinking with God's Word. Meditating regularly on it is an indispensable key to accomplishing this.

Scripture exhorts us to meditate on various aspects of God and his Word so that our knowledge of him is all-embracing and we are equipped for every situation we face in life. For example:

'Oh, how I love your law! I meditate on it all day long.'
(Psalm 119:97)

'On my bed I remember you; I think of you through the watches of the night.'
(Psalm 63:6)

'I will meditate on all your works and consider all your mighty deeds.'
(Psalm 77:12)

'My eyes stay open through the watches of the night, that I may meditate on your promises.'
(Psalm 119:148)

Note that meditation is something that we can do all day and all night. As we do this God's Word finds an abiding place in our hearts and minds (John 15:7). You will effectively maintain your faith image as you turn this vital key. In addition, God promises prosperity and success to those who meditate on and put into practice his Word:

'Do not let this Book of the Law depart from your mouth; meditate on it day and night, so that you may be careful to do everything written in it. Then you will be prosperous and successful.'
(Joshua 1:8)

While meditating, memorise key scriptures - specific promises - that God highlights to you. This may be a discipline at first but the benefits you reap will encourage you to continue.

9. The Tracks Don't Fit

As the years pass, the ruts in the long track to the farm become deeper by the constant use of heavy farm vehicles in all weathers. The farmer has a large four-wheel-drive vehicle which fits the deep ruts perfectly, enabling him to drive up and down the track easily. But when visitors in smaller cars arrive, it is a long, slow and bumpy ride up to the farm - especially for three-wheeled vehicles!

Imagine your mind is the farm road. Before you came to Christ ungodly thoughts slipped regularly along it, cutting deep tracks like those made by the farm vehicles. Now that you are a Christian, all things are new. A new owner (Christ) with new vehicles (godly thoughts) now use the track. At first it seems hard going but eventually the new vehicles cut fresh ruts into the track. The previous owner's vehicles (evil thoughts) now have a rough ride whereas the new owner's vehicles pass easily along it.

You must drive God's Word and wholesome thoughts up and down the tracks of your mind until they become the first thing you think of in every situation. Evil thoughts, on the other hand, will become so uncomfortable in the tracks of your mind that they will be immediately exposed for what they are!

'You were taught, with regard to your former way of life, to put off your old self, which is being corrupted by its deceitful desires; to be made new in the attitude of your minds; and to put on the new self.'
(Ephesians 4:22-24)

10. Doing the Word

Maintaining your faith image is not only an issue of thinking correctly and winning the battles for your mind - it also depends on your practical obedience to God's Word on a daily basis.

a. Deeds

Faith must be accompanied by deeds to be real faith.

'Faith by itself, if it is not accompanied by action, is dead ... Show me your faith without deeds, and I will show you my faith by what I do.'
(James 2:17-18)

b. Obedience

Faith in God's Word results in obedience.

'We received grace and apostleship to call people from among all the Gentiles to the obedience that comes from faith.'
(Romans 1:5)

c. Perseverance

Faith in God's Word produces perseverance.

'You need to persevere so that when you have done the will of God, you will receive what he has promised.'
(Hebrews 10:36)

Building your life wisely demands that you both hear and do God's Word (Matthew 7:24-27). As you respond obediently each day to God's word to you, you not only maintain your faith image but start to bring it into being!

11. Conclusion

Stay motivated by God's Word, the Bible, and by his word to you. Refresh your mind with it; let it stimulate you to wholesome thinking; meditate on it; memorise it; and most importantly, do it:

'being confident of this, that he who began a good work in you will carry it on to completion until the day of Christ Jesus.'
(Philippians 1:6)

LESSON 5

Group Discussion Questions

1. Discuss what it means to meditate on God's Word both day and night.

2. How do you maintain your faith image when circumstances around you seem to worsen?

3. Share how you have coped successfully with the delay between God giving you a word of faith and you seeing its fulfilment (for example, Abraham's twenty-five-year wait for Isaac).

4. How do you practically refresh your memory with God's Word?

5. What part does practical obedience play in maintaining your faith image?

Personal Application

1. A mind filled with the Word of God is the key to maintaining your faith image through any period of time. Cultivate a right attitude to God's Word by:

   a. Reading Psalm 119 and highlighting/underlining every reference to God's Word (law, commands, statutes, precepts, etc).

   b. List the attitudes David expresses in this Psalm towards God's Word.

   c. Ask God to open his Word to you in a new way as you approach it in the same way as David does in this Psalm.

2. Memorise Hebrews 6:12.

NOTES

Lesson 6
THINKING AS GOD THINKS

'"No eye has seen, no ear has heard, no mind has conceived what God has prepared for those who love him" - but God has revealed it to us by his Spirit ... "For who has known the mind of the Lord that he may instruct him?" But we have the mind of Christ.'
(1 Corinthians 2:9-10, 16)

1. We Have the Mind of Christ

To become Christ-like we must think like Christ for, as a man *'thinks within himself, so he is' (Proverbs 23:7 NASB)*. How, then, can we think like God? How can a finite mind tap into the infinite wisdom of God? The very concept seems inconceivable! Yet God tells us, *'We have the mind of Christ' (1 Corinthians 2:16)*.

This statement of fact means that we can actually think God's thoughts. We can react and speak as he would and be a party to the deep mysteries of God. But how can this be?

2. The Old and the New

Under the old covenant, people came to know the mind of God by observing a written code. The law expressed the heart and mind of God and by keeping it they came to understand something of his heart and mind. It taught them the rights and wrongs of God's standard and helped them to live godly lives - yet it was merely external. Nothing from within them prompted or guided them into God's way or gave them insight into the mind of God.

This all changed with the coming of Christ and the establishing of the new covenant between God and man.

'"The time is coming," declares the Lord, "when I will make a new covenant with the house of Israel and with the house of Judah ... This is the covenant that I will make with the house of Israel after that time," declares the Lord. "I will put my law in their minds and write it on their hearts. I will be their God, and they will be my people."'
(Jeremiah 31:31, 33)

God's law is no longer written on stone tablets or in a textbook merely to be learned - it is written in your mind and on your heart. It is an ever-present internal resource to teach and guide you in every situation of life.

3. God's Spirit in You

At the point of your salvation the Holy Spirit took up residence in your life. You were *'born of the Spirit' (John 3:5)* and the ongoing work of the Spirit within you is what now marks you out as a Christian:

'Having believed, you were marked in him with a seal, the promised Holy Spirit.'
(Ephesians 1:13)

Understanding the work of the Holy Spirit within you will help you see that you really do have the mind of Christ.

a. The Spirit knows the mind of God

'The Spirit searches all things, even the deep things of God. For who among men knows the thoughts of a man except the man's spirit within him? In the same way no-one knows the thoughts of God except the Spirit of God. We have not received the spirit of the world but the Spirit who is from God, that we may understand what God has freely given us.'
(1 Corinthians 2:10-12)

The same Spirit who knows 'even the deep things of God' now lives in you! This gives you access to these same 'deep things'. By the Spirit in you, you have the mind of Christ. That is why Paul can also say:

'"No eye has seen, no ear has heard, no mind has conceived what God has prepared for those who love him" - but God has revealed it to us by his Spirit.'
(1 Corinthians 2:9-10)

Things that no natural mind can comprehend or understand are shown to us by the Spirit. Why? So that we might:

'Realise and comprehend and appreciate the gifts (of divine favour and blessing so freely and lavishly) bestowed on us by God.'
(1 Corinthians 2:12 Amplified)

b. The Spirit leads us into truth

Jesus said: *'I am ... the truth'* (John 14:6). Then, in speaking of the work of the Spirit in the lives of his followers, he said:

'When he, the Spirit of truth, comes, he will guide you into all truth ... All that belongs to the Father is mine. That is why I said the Spirit will take from what is mine and make it known to you.'
(John 16:13, 15)

The Spirit takes of Christ's heart and mind and reveals it to us. So within us we have a directional force guiding us into the ways of Christ and revealing his heart to us concerning every matter we face in life. The apostle John also equated our knowledge of God's truth with the work of the indwelling Holy Spirit:

'You have an anointing from the Holy One, and all of you know the truth.'
(1 John 2:20)

Because of the Holy Spirit living in us, we have the mind of Christ. Now we'll look at how this principle works in our daily living.

4. The Inner Witness

The directive work of the Holy Spirit is often described as the 'inner witness' or 'inner prompting'. I recently spoke to a new Christian who understood little of God's ways yet somehow felt it was wrong to sleep with his girlfriend now that he was a Christian. Consequently, he stopped. I was able to confirm to him from God's Word that this was God's will. What had happened? He had been guided into God's way by the inner prompting of the Spirit. The Holy Spirit had led him into the truth.

Probably the best way to describe this inner feeling is as a peace or dispeace about any specific issue. In writing to the church at Colossae, Paul said:

'Let the peace of Christ rule in your hearts, since as members of one body you were called to peace.'
(Colossians 3:15)

Another version translates this verse:

'Let the peace (soul harmony which comes) from the Christ rule (act as umpire continually) in your hearts - deciding and settling with finality all questions that arise in your minds.'
(Colossians 3:15 Amplified)

Paul is describing the work of the Spirit within us. When an issue arises about which we are uncertain and a battle rages in our mind, we should ask ourselves: 'If I do this, will I still feel God's peace filling my heart?' If so, do it; if not, don't!

5. Safety Factor

Whether the Spirit prompts you positively or negatively, you can expect his direction to be confirmed by the Bible, because God's Word is 'the word of truth' *(Ephesians 1:13; Colossians 1:5)*. Thus the Spirit and the Word together are inseparable and constitute God's safety factor for us.

When we hear God's Word, the Spirit confirms it with his peace. When the Spirit prompts us to act, the Word of God will confirm it.

Acting without the assurance that God's Spirit and the Bible agree on an issue can lead us into error. Swayed by emotion rather than the Spirit, some have become involved in wrong practices because they felt that God was telling them to do a certain thing. If you feel it, check it with the Word.

For example, I recall speaking to a young man who felt that God was telling him to date a non-Christian girl. He had to be helped to understand that the normal purpose of such a relationship is to culminate in marriage and that God's Word precludes marriage to a non-Christian:

'Do not be yoked together with unbelievers. For what do righteousness and wickedness have in common? Or what fellowship can light have with darkness?'
(2 Corinthians 6:14)

God would not direct this young man by the Spirit to do anything that was contrary to his Word.

Then sometimes it works the other way round. For example I recall in my own life finding things in the Bible which did not fit in with the theology of my particular denominational background. My mind rejected them - but the Spirit seemed to urge me to reconsider. The Spirit of God was provoking me to see that God wanted me to live in the good of all his Word, not just the sections that suited my particular brand of theology. The Spirit was confirming the Word of God to me.

6. Conscience

In conjunction with the peace of God that rules in our hearts and guides us into God's ways, the Spirit also uses our conscience. This is the inner affirmation of our conduct which proceeds out of our accumulated knowledge of what is right and wrong. Conscience literally means 'with knowledge' and is educated by our background, upbringing and education. Everybody has one as a human being but they are not all educated equally, which is why some people's conscience allows them to do things that another person would have a 'guilty conscience' about. The Christian's conscience is also educated by the Holy Spirit, reading God's Word and an environment of church and Christian friends. This is why our conscience stops us doing things that our non-Christian friends do with a clear conscience.

Your conscience is like a red warning light on a car dashboard. It comes on to warn you that you are about to run into trouble if you don't stop and remedy the fault. Another common phrase that people use to describe their conscience is: 'My warning bells rang.' For the Christian, it is God's Spirit in you that rings them!

To keep you walking in God's truth, the Spirit confirms that an action is wrong by giving you pangs of conscience. Equally, as right decisions are made, you have a good or clear conscience - an inner knowledge that you are doing right.

a. Your conscience confirms God's law written in your heart

'The requirements of the law are written on their hearts, their consciences also bearing witness.'
(Romans 2:15)

b. Your conscience confirms the words you speak

'I speak the truth in Christ - I am not lying, my conscience confirms it in the Holy Spirit.'
(Romans 9:1)

c. Your conscience confirms the way you conduct yourself

'This is our boast: Our conscience testifies that we have conducted ourselves in the world, and especially in our relations with you, in the holiness and sincerity that are from God.'
(2 Corinthians 1:12)

It is the grace of God that he gave us his Spirit to lead us into his ways. Through the operation of the inner prompting of the Spirit, your conscience and God's Word, you will think God's thoughts. You will know his mind on all matters and think, speak and act as he would, for you 'have the mind of Christ' (1 Corinthians 2:16).

7. Know Him to Think Like Him

'I want to know Christ and the power of his resurrection.'
(Philippians 3:10)

The more you get to know God the more you will understand why his Spirit leads you as he does. A growing knowledge of his nature and character is vital as a foundation to understanding his ways and thus his thoughts. Sometimes our natural reasoning seems good - but the mind of Christ in us tells us otherwise!

To illustrate this, we will briefly look at just one facet of God's nature to see how radically it affects the way he thinks. Knowing the nature of your God will help you to see things through his eyes.

8. God's Plumb Line

'The Lord is righteous, he loves justice; upright men will see his face.'
(Psalm 11:7)

God is righteous. He always thinks and speaks what is right and just. No error or untruth is found in him; he is without sin and abhors it. In his dealings with men he is therefore totally righteous.

At a time when God was speaking strongly to the proud, complacent and rebellious in Israel, he prophetically stated that he was establishing a standard among them so that in future they would have no excuse for their sins:

'The Lord was standing by a wall that had been built true to plumb, with a plumb line in his hand. And the Lord asked me, "What do you see, Amos?" "A plumb line," I replied. Then the Lord said, "Look, I am setting a plumb line among my people Israel; I will spare them no longer."'
(Amos 7:7-8)

God was establishing a plumb line, a clear standard for men to see. But what was that plumb line? Isaiah explains:

'I lay a stone in Zion, a tested stone, a precious cornerstone for a sure foundation; the one who trusts will never be dismayed. I will make justice the measuring line and righteousness the plumb line.'
(Isaiah 28:16-17)

Righteousness is God's plumb line. In the above scripture God is speaking prophetically about the church. Christ is the 'cornerstone' (1 Peter 2:4-6), and the building composed of living stones, representing the church, will only be constructed properly if it is built true to plumb, in other words in righteousness.

We are the church. Our lives must therefore be built in accordance with God's righteous plumb line. Understanding this helps us to understand how God thinks about all that we do with our lives.

Through believing in Christ we have been made righteous.

'This righteousness from God comes through faith in Jesus Christ to all who believe.'
(Romans 3:22)

'God made him who had no sin to be sin for us, so that in him we might become the righteousness of God.'
(2 Corinthians 5:21)

This is the condition God sees us in and the position from which his Spirit in us views all things. Therefore, in thinking about all we do, God's Spirit and his Word will guide us along the righteous path. It will not include sin of any description. It will cause us to speak righteously to all men; relate righteously with our families, friends, employers and even our enemies; act righteously in every situation we face; and have a righteous attitude in all that we do.

9. Black and White

God deals in absolutes and righteousness is one of them. There is no middle ground between what is righteous and what is unrighteous. We see this truth reflected in the way God describes the condition in which mankind can be found. People are either dead or alive (Ephesians 2:1-5), lost or found (Luke 15:8-10), in darkness or in light (Ephesians 5:8).

As he looks into the affairs of this world and our individual lives, he sees no grey areas. In God's mind there are no fences to sit on - we are either on one side or the other! This should be reflected in the way we think, because we have the mind of Christ. Since we think God's thoughts, our lives will be very distinct from the lives of those who are unrighteous:

'You will again see the distinction between the righteous and the wicked, between those who serve God and those who do not.'
(Malachi 3:18)

10. Now the Battle's Won!

What a privilege it is to be able to think as God thinks! Determine to make time to meditate on God's nature and character. Then let it fill your mind and invade your whole being, because the way you think is the way you'll become.

A sure sign that the battle for the mind is won is progressive change into Christlikeness. The fruit of victory is seen in your life. Satan's tricks and lies are quickly recognised, refused and replaced with God's Word. You are filling your mind with God's thoughts, adopting his perspective on all matters and issues of life. You are indeed able to declare like the apostle John:

'We will have confidence on the day of judgment, because in this world we are like him.'
(1 John 4:17)

LESSON 6

Group Discussion Questions

1. How do we distinguish between the mind of Christ in us and our own, sometimes wrong, thought patterns?

2. How important is it that the Bible agrees with what we feel in our spirit God is prompting us to do?

3. Share individually how you have learned to hear and obey the inner prompting of the Spirit.

Personal Application

1. Meditate on the significance of the truth that you have 'the mind of Christ' (1 Corinthians 2:16).

2. Make a list of as many aspects of God's nature as you can think of (e.g. righteous, all powerful, hates sin, cannot lie). Select one or two and, with the help of a concordance and perhaps a Christian friend, study these particular aspects of the nature of God.

3. Identify any aspects of your life which the Holy Spirit is asking you to deal with or change. Respond to his promptings and walk with a clear conscience.

Full details of other resources by Stephen Matthew are available from:

Abundant Life Church
Wapping Road, Bradford
West Yorkshire BD3 0EQ

Tel: +44 (0)1274 307233
Fax: +44 (0)1274 740698
Email: admin@alm.org.uk

For a copy of our free quarterly magazine
'Voice to the Nations' please contact us as above.

Visit our online store at **www.alm.org.uk**

Browse the full range of preaching, teaching, training, music
and worship resources available from Abundant Life Ministries

---

Other book titles available from Abundant Life Resources:

It's Not Over 'Till The Barren Woman Sings
by Paul Scanlon

Crossing Over
by Paul Scanlon

Consumer or Consumed?
by Charlotte Scanlon-Gambill

The Battle For The Loins
by Paul Scanlon

NOTES

NOTES